Sandbagger's
Handbook

A Guide to Making Money on the
Golf Course the Easy Way

Bob Peck
and
Sandy Silver

Andrews and McMeel
A Universal Press Syndicate Company
Kansas City

The Official Sandbagger's Handbook: A Guide to Making Money on the Golf Course the Easy Way copyright © 1997 by Action Publishing and Marketing, Inc. and Bob Peck and Sandy Silver. All rights reserved. Printed in the United States of America. No part of this book may be used or reproduced in any manner whatsoever without written permission except in the case of reprints in the context of reviews. For information, write Andrews and McMeel, a Universal Press Syndicate Company, 4520 Main Street, Kansas City, Missouri 64111.

ISBN: 0-8362-2761-1

Library of Congress Catalog Card Number: 96-86689

ATTENTION: SCHOOLS AND BUSINESSES

Andrews and McMeel books are available at quantity discounts with bulk purchase for educational, business, or sales promotional use. For information, please write to: Special Sales Department, Andrews and McMeel, 4520 Main Street, Kansas City, Missouri 64111.

Sand • bag • ger *n*

1: *Archaic* a highway-man who preyed on travelers using a long, tubelike sack filled with sand 2: a golfer who commits highway rob-bery using his handi-cap as a lethal weapon

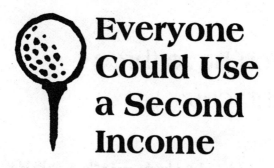

Everyone
Could Use
a Second
Income

You have three
choices:

1. Work the night shift
   at your local Stop &
   Rob.

2. Try the latest net-
work marketing deal
—a soap that not
only gets you clean,
but if you eat it, it will
flush your toxins and
give you renewed
vigor.

· · · · · · · · · · · · · · · · · ·

3. Or . . . you can play
   golf, take money
   from people who
   really don't need it
   . . . and get a tan in
   the process.

· · · · · · · · · · · · · · · · ·

Now that you have chosen number three, sit back, relax, and absorb the money-making principles we have detailed in this handbook.

Warning: For important tax advice, please consult with your CPA.

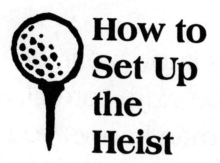

How to Set Up the Heist

If you know your victim, be extra careful. This man knows your modus operandi. He also knows your real handicap.

• • • • • • • • • • • • • • • • •

Best strategy:

Whine about not having played recently.

• • • • • • • • • • • • • • • • •

Second-best strategy:

Beg for strokes.

Identifying a
Victim

If your victim simply appears before you on the golf course, say "Thank you, God." Then go introduce yourself, and don't forget to mention that you have never played this golf course before.

Identifying a victim:

1. He's new in town.

2. He's taking the whole golf thing a little too seriously.

3. He smells like
money.

Warning: None of these suggestions works if his name is painted on his bag.

What to
Wear . . .
What to
Wear . . .

Your first impression is made within the first thirty seconds of meeting the victim. You must make him feel superior. Encourage him by dressing down.

Fashion Tips:

1. Accentuate the negative—think nerd.

● ● ● ● ● ● ● ● ● ● ● ● ● ● ● ●

2. Polyester is preferred. Go to secondhand shops if necessary.

3. Make a fashion statement; bad hats are good.

4. Stripes with plaids
are fabulous.

5. Footwear: Learn to play in sneakers.

6. Socks are optional.

7. If you see someone
   you know, tell him
   you didn't have time
   to do the laundry.

Equipment
and
Accessories

If you have to have
good equipment, then
you must act like you
don't know how to
use it.

Suggestions:

1. Don't carry a one iron.

2. Have a newish bag . . . lots of bag tags . . . and a pull cart.

3. Use funny animal head covers.

4. Wear gloves on both hands.

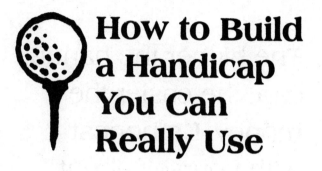

How to Build
a Handicap
You Can
Really Use

The higher the handicap, the easier the money. Be honest with yourself about your true handicap . . . then double it!!

In order to establish
your new *inflated*
handicap:

1. Play winter golf . . .
   it's easy to lose balls
   in the snow.

2. Drink heavily, but not so much you forget to count every stroke.

3. Play hurt.

4. Get a divorce . . . or declare bankruptcy.

5. Before each tee shot, visualize your wife with Richard Gere.

6. Before each putt,
visualize yourself
with Roseanne.

7. Wear underwear that's one size too small.

8. Watch tapes of
   Gerald Ford at the
   Bob Hope Classic.

9. Annoy yourself on purpose: Listen to Michael Bolton tapes while you play.

10. Spread the double bogeys around your scorecard as evenly as possible . . . think of it as pollinating your handicap.

11. If, in spite of these suggestions, you should happen to accidentally shoot a good score, eat your scorecard. Leave no evidence.

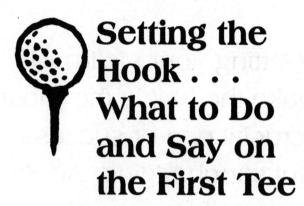

Setting the Hook . . . What to Do and Say on the First Tee

Getting your victim to take the bait is the most crucial part of successful sandbagging. Apply yourself for five minutes, then count your money for the next four hours.

Critical moves:

1. Introduction—let him shake hands with a limp fish. Mention that it was such a nice day you just had to "go golfing."

2. Take some bad-looking practice swings. Try to copy Miller Barber.

3. Language: "I played the funnest game last week for the first time. I believe it was called 'Skins.'"

4. Follow-up:
"Unfortunately, I
didn't do so well,
but I'd like to learn
more about it."

5. Follow-up number
   two: "I haven't been
   on my game since
   my last back
   surgery."

6. Sucking up works. Mention the coordination of his outfit, the outstanding quality of his clubs, and the magnificence of his practice swing. Suck up more if you need to.

7. Next: After you've
   confirmed his handi-
   cap and established
   how much the Skins
   are worth, pull out
   your little laminated
   USGA card that lists
   you as a thirty handi-
   cap and confirm
   your nerd status.

8. Try not to show your
pleasure. We advise
against drooling.

Keeping the Scam Going . . . What to Say During Play

Now that you're on the highway to easy money, turn on the cruise control.

Effective bullshit:

1. Flatter your victim unmercifully. After he makes a two-foot putt, say, "That one was a lot harder than it looked."

2. "How long have you
   been playing this
   well?"

3. After he hits a bad shot: "I saw Jack Nicklaus miss that same shot."

4. "Did you play for your college team?"

5. "Have you ever thought of turning pro?"

6. "John Daly has nothing on you."

7. "Your putting stroke reminds me of the Crenshaw video."

8. After he misses
another green, say,
"These yardages
must be off."

9. Apologize sincerely and often for your own good shots: "I never hit shots like that. I should play with you more often."

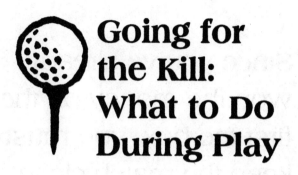

Going for the Kill:
What to Do
During Play

Since you've already
won the money on the
first tee box, you must
keep the match close
and look foolish
enough doing it so that:

A. He'll pay you.

B. He'll come back for more.

Best strategies:

1. Waggle a lot.

2. Swing hard and whiff.

3. Push the tee into the ground with your thumb.

4. Be indecisive about which club to hit.

5. Mark your scorecard
   before you exit the
   green.

6. When losing a hole, make it something he'll remember . . . like a quadruple bogey. Take your time with every shot. Appear intense.

General Sandbagger Strategy: Enhance Your Earning Power

You've got the basics.
Here are some points
to help you fine tune
"the sting":

1. Public golf courses—
   more nerd freedom.
   An abundance of re-
   tirees means social
   security money and
   their kids' inheritances
   are available. Note:
   Find a victim who
   wants to play for more
   than nickel Skins.

2. Private golf courses: Flocks of fat pigeons begging to be plucked. Big egos and medium-sized handicaps are a wonderful combination. Caution: Watch your flank. Clubs are full of guys with the same evil scheme.

3. How to protect your reputation: Wear dark sunglasses, avoid photographers, and use a one-word alias like "Slim" or "Buddy."

4. Develop a bad-looking swing that works . . . think of Boy George playing tennis . . . naked!

• • • • • • • • • • • • • • • •

5. Tournament sand-
bagging: Announce
your handicap like
the proud father of
an ugly kid.
Reinforce your nerd
appeal by continu-
ally going up to the
tournament director
or pro and asking,

• • • • • • • • • • • • • • • •

"Where do we go now?" When they hand you the trophy, show some emotion. Imagine a world with no beer.

Proper Nineteenth-Hole Etiquette: Making a Clean Getaway

You've pummeled the poor guy into submission. Now it's time to be gracious and set him up for next time.

Closing arguments:

1. When the scores are tallied and you have won, feign surprise and disbelief. Say, "Holy shit. Are you kidding me?"

2. When he coughs up
a big wad of cash,
be humble. Say, "I'd
better enjoy this
while I can, 'cause
I know you will beat
me next time."

3. Devote a percentage of the winnings to the liquor tab. Think of this as an investment in your future.